The Cow Says Moo

****

Ten Tips to Teach Toddlers to Talk:

An Early Intervention Guide

****

ALSO BY THIS AUTHOR

(As Anita Shannon)

Toddler Talk: Consonants

Toddler Talk: Consonants and Digraphs

Toddler Talk: Vowels

Toddler Talk: Consonant-Vowel Words

The Baby Owl Says Hoo

The Cow Says Moo

****

Ten Tips to Teach Toddlers to Talk:

An Early Intervention Guide

****

Vicky McErLean, M.S.Ed.

with Madelyn Bythell

ISBN-13: 978-1482794403
ISBN-10: 1482794403

About the Authors

Vicky McErlean has a Master of Science in Education. She is certified in the areas of early childhood education, elementary education, and special education, and is pursuing certification as a Board Certified Behavior Analyst. She has worked as an independent consultant, providing home-based special instruction to children from diverse backgrounds and with various impairments and developmental delays. In her current employment, Ms. McErlean often identifies and refers children with speech and language disorders, cognitive impairment, sensory integration dysfunction, and autistic spectrum disorder. She consults and co-treats with other professionals in the field of early intervention, including occupational therapists, speech and language pathologists, and medical professionals. As an early-intervention provider, she has received numerous commendations from the families she has served.

Madelyn Bythell has been a professional technical communicator for more than 25 years. She currently works for a major software company.

Table of Contents

Introduction: Is My Child Delayed?

Children generally begin using words on the following schedule:

Age	Communication
6 months	Babble
9 months	Uses four different syllables (such as *ba, ma, da, na*) Can combine two syllables (such as *mama* or *baba*)
12 months	Says one or two words spontaneously Says *mama* and *dada* specifically
15 months	Has a spontaneous vocabulary of about 10 words
18 months	Has 15 meaningful words
21 months	Can imitate two and three word phrases (such as *uh oh, oh no*) Can use single-word sentences
2 years	Has about 50 words Begins to use pronouns (I, you, me)
2.5 years	Uses three-word sentences Can give their full name when asked
3 years	Can relate personal experiences Can converse in sentences (4+ words) Can answer "what," "where," and "who" questions Has a vocabulary of at least 200 words

Most children learn to speak on their own without direct assistance. Even children who are slow to speak early on typically catch up to their peers by the age of three. Unfortunately, there is no way for parents, educators, or health-care professionals to know in advance which children will catch up and which children will not.

About This Book

Fortunately, parents can easily be proactive by using this book as a teaching tool and guide to helping toddlers develop their language skills.

- **Tip 1: Do What Does Not Come Naturally** shows you how to give your child a reason to talk.

- **Tip 2: Juice or Milk?** explains how to provide your child with more opportunities to expand his language skills.

- **Tip 3: Simple Signs** explains how you can use sign language to help your child make the connection that language has a purpose.

- **Tip 4: Be Silly** shows you how to incorporate silliness into everyday situations in order to promote listening skills.

- **Tip 5: Talk It Out!** explains how verbalizing your own actions and those of your child expose your child to different aspects of language, speech, and communication.

- **Tip 6: Keep It Moving!** explains how you can use oral motor exercises in order to help your child practice the mouth movements that are vital for speech.

- **Tip 7: The Cow Says Moo** shows you how to help your child find the right word.

- **Tip 8: Break It Down** shows you how to break words down into smaller components so that your child can communicate more effectively.

- **Tip 9: Get Your Groove On** shows you how to pair movement with sound in order to help your child learn language through a sensation other than sound.

- **Tip 10: Books, Books, and More Books** shows you how to incorporate books into your strategy for encouraging language development.

While Using This Guide

Keep in mind that your child's response depends on skills in all areas of development. Speech does not develop in isolation. It is influenced by motor, social, emotional, adaptive, and cognitive development. Moreover, not all techniques are effective for all children. Don't be discouraged if your child fails to respond to a particular technique. He might need more time or a different technique might be better suited for his developmental skills.

What This Book Is Not

This book does not replace therapeutic or medical treatment. If you are concerned about your child's development, consult with your pediatrician, neurologist, audiologist, or other specialist. In addition, you can contact your local Early Intervention Program administrator (see Appendix 7 and Appendix 8) for additional support.

Safety Notice

I cannot stress enough the importance of ensuring your child's safety. Some of the techniques described throughout this book suggest the use of small objects that can be choking hazards. In rare cases, your child might even be sensitive or even allergic to a suggested product. For these reasons, you must remain in control of the activity at all times.

You Are Not Alone

This guide empowers you to help your child. The exercises should not create undue stress. Praise your child's efforts to communicate, no matter how slight. His emotional development is just as important as any other skill. If you feel discouraged at a perceived lack of progress, seek additional assistance from a health-care professional.

Not Just for Parents

This guide is designed primarily for use by parents, but it can also be an effective resource tool for use by other family members, teachers, childcare providers, and health-care professionals.

Tip 1: Do What Does Not Come Naturally

Do not handicap your children by making their lives easy. — Robert A. Heinlein

At a holiday party several years ago, my sister was holding her daughter on her lap. When someone asked how old my niece was, my sister responded, "Eighteen months." When the woman said "Oh, not a baby anymore then," my sister gasped aloud, never having considered that her daughter was no longer a 'baby'.

In fact, children transition relatively quickly from infant to toddler. So, that tiny little being who was completely dependent on you for her every need is now quite capable of making her desires known through actions, gestures, and words.

If your child is not yet using words to communicate, consider that *you* might not have made the same transition. You might still be doing what has become second nature—anticipating her needs. Unfortunately, this behavior can hinder language development in a toddler.

So, tip number one is this: Do what does *not* come naturally. Stop anticipating your child's needs. Give your child a reason to talk.

Example

During mealtime, eighteen-month-old Kayla's mother puts only a small amount of a favorite food on Kayla's plate. Kayla eats the small portion of food but does not attempt to communicate that she would like more. Here are some other possible responses:

- Kayla eats the small portion of food and then attempts to communicate verbally that she wants more.

- Kayla eats the small portion of food and then attempts to communicate that she wants more by pointing or gesturing, but she does not vocalize.

- Kayla eats the small portion of food, and then has a screaming tantrum to indicate that she wants more.

Now, consider the table at the beginning of this book (**Introduction: Is My Child Delayed?**). Is Kayla's response appropriate for her age? If not, there are many opportunities that Kayla's mother can incorporate throughout her day in order to encourage speech.

Now, consider how your own child might respond in a similar situation. If your child's response is not appropriate for his age, then choose which of the opportunities listed in this chapter would be best to include into *your* daily routines.

Tip Guidelines

Before you begin, here are three guidelines to follow when using this tip to encourage speech.

- If you don't get the response that you are looking for within a few seconds, show him the response that you are looking for, and then give him what he wants before frustration ensues.

- Don't tell her when it is time to speak. She might become dependent on your command.

- Be like Goldilocks and look for the response that is "just right." Think back to the example with Kayla. Kayla did not give her mother any indication that she wanted more food. For eighteen-month-old Kayla, a gesture or sign would be "just right." Now, consider your own child's age. For example, while he is playing with blocks, one of the following responses is "just right":

    - a gesture or sign (see **Tip 3: Simple Signs)**

    - an initial sound (*buh*)

    - a word approximation (*ba, bok, ook*)

    - a true word (*block*)

    - multiple words (*big block, build block, blue block, block please*)

Language-Development Opportunities

Here are some examples of how to incorporate this language-development tip throughout your day.

Daily Routines - In, Out, Up, Down, Open, Help, Done

- Place snacks in clear, sealed bags to encourage your child to ask for *help* or request that you *open* the bag.

- When entering or exiting a room with a closed door, stand by the door and ask, "*What do you want?*" Demonstrate words such as *open* or *out*.

- When mealtime is over, do not immediately remove your child from his highchair. Instead, take the opportunity to encourage the use of such words as *done, out, down*.

- When your child puts his arms up to be picked up, encourage him to say *up*. Likewise, encourage him to tell you when he wants to be put *down*.

Organization and Design

- Obstacles can be opportunities! You are probably already using cabinet and refrigerator locks. If you are not already doing so, put juice boxes and snacks behind these locks. In this way, you are motivating your child to ask for a treat.

- Place toys in clear, plastic storage bins to urge your child to request a specific toy. This is also an opportunity to promote the use of words such as *help* and *open*.

Playtime

- During turn-taking games, such as rolling a ball or car back and forth, after your child rolls the ball to you, encourage him to use words or phrases such as *me, I do,* or *my turn*.

Bonus! Placing toys in bins also helps your child learn sorting, categorizing, and cleaning up!

- For games with multiple pieces, such as peg puzzles, blocks, or shape sorters, give your child only one piece at a time, motivating her to ask for more. Depending on her skill level, you might expect specific labels for each piece (for example, *circle, square, dog, cat*). You also might expect one word to represent all pieces (for example, *puzzle, shape, block*).

- On the playground, wait to be asked before pushing him on the swing or down the slide.

Tip 2: Juice or Milk?

The strongest principle of growth lies in human choice. — *George Eliot*

As parents, we tend to ask our children yes and no questions, such as *"Are you done?,"* or *"Do you want a cookie?"* By limiting our child's response to yes or no, a headshake, or a nod, we limit the demand for language.

So, tip number two is this: Give your child the opportunity to make a choice. Choices provide your child with more opportunities to practice his language skills. They also allow him to feel as if he has some control over his environment (which can help thwart tantrums!).

Example

Twenty-four-month-old Michael pulls his mother to the refrigerator because he wants something to drink. Michael's mother opens the refrigerator, removes both the juice and milk containers, and asks Michael, *"Do you want juice or milk?"* Michael points to the juice. His mother reinforces his choice by saying the word *"juice."* Here are some examples of other possible responses:

- Michael vocalizes his choice (*juice, ja, oose*).

- Michael looks at the choice but does nothing.

- Michael has a screaming tantrum when asked to convey his choice.

Now, consider the table at the beginning of this book (**Introduction: Is My Child Delayed?**). Is Michael's response appropriate for his age? If not, there are many opportunities that his mother can incorporate throughout her day in order to encourage speech.

Now, consider how your own child might respond in a similar situation. If your child's response is not appropriate for his age, then choose which of the opportunities listed in this chapter would be best to include into *your* daily routines.

Tip Guidelines

Before you begin, here are some guidelines to follow when using this tip to encourage speech.

- Offer only what you are willing to give. Don't offer him a choice between juice and milk, if you are not willing to let him drink juice.

- Mix up the order in which you present the choice. If your child has a receptive language delay, he might always pick the first choice that he hears. Alternatively, he might always pick the last choice because it is the most fresh in his memory.

- Help your child be successful, even if it just means helping him point to or touch his choice.

Language-Development Opportunities

Here are some examples of how to incorporate this language-development tip throughout your day.

Family Meals and Snack-Time

- Food choices

- Drink choices

- Type of seating (for example, booster or highchair)

- Location of seat (for example, next to Mommy or Daddy)

- Cup choice (for example, straw or sippy, choice between colors, choice between favorites)

- Bowl choice

Clothing

- Color of clothing

- Type of clothing (for example, long pants versus shorts, skirt versus pants)

- Choice between favorite characters on clothing

- Choice between what to put on first

- Types of footwear

Television/Video/DVD

- Choice between favorite shows

- Type of seating (for example, chair, couch, floor, bed)

- Room location

At the Playground

- Slide or swing

- Under or over

- Up or down

- First or second

- Fast or slow

- My Turn or Your Turn

Games and Activities

- Shape sorters: choice between shapes

- Puzzles: choice of piece

- Animals, balls, blocks, cars: choice of size, color, texture, type, name

- Turn-taking: choice of who goes first

- Choice of books, songs, or nursery rhymes

- Arts and crafts: color or paint, brush or fingers, paper or coloring book, glue stick or squeeze glue, markers or crayons

- Gross motor activities: jumping, marching, dancing, spinning, wheelbarrow walking

Bath and Bed Time

- Bath or shower

- Sponge versus washcloth

- Type of bath toy

- Color of towel

- Type of sleepwear

Tip 3: Simple Signs

A warm smile is the universal language of kindness. — William Arthur Ward

In learning to ask for what they want, whether by using signs or spoken words, children learn that language is functional. This connection is a crucial step in the process of language development. The goal of teaching your child to sign is not to replace speech but to help your child make the connection that language means something.

So, tip number three is this: Use sign language to help your child make the connection that using language serves a purpose.

Tip Guidelines

Before you begin, here are guidelines to follow when using this tip to encourage speech.

- Start with words that both represent activities and items in which your child is interested *and* that have signs that are clearly distinct from one another. Some words that have distinct signs are *puzzle piece, car,* and *cookie.* Two words that have similar signs are *ball* and *movie.*

- Avoid introducing too many signs at once. Start with three to five distinct signs for highly preferred items such as a favorite activity (music, TV), toy (ball, car, animal), snack (cookie, chip), or drink (juice, milk).

For sign instructions, refer to **Appendix 2: Simple Signs for Toddlers.**

Techniques to Teaching a Sign

1. Direct your child's attention toward a desired item.

2. When she reaches for or looks at the item, ask, *"What do you want?"* and then proceed quickly through steps 3-5.

3. Say the name of the item while simultaneously demonstrating the sign.

4. Repeat the name of the item while you are helping her imitate the sign.

5. Demonstrate the sign again and say the name of the item while handing it to her.

Example

It's snack time and Robert's mother is working on teaching her son the sign for cookie. She puts several small bite-sized cookie pieces in a bowl out of Robert's reach and then directs his attention toward the cookies (Step 1).

When Robert reaches for the cookies, his mom asks, "*What do you want?*" (Step 2) and then quickly says and signs "*cookie*" (Step 3). Next, she repeats "*cookie*" while helping Robert imitate the sign (Step 4). She finishes by demonstrating the sign again and quickly handing the cookies to Robert while saying "*cookie*" (Step 5).

The ultimate goal is for your child to request the item when it is not in sight. When he begins to sign without full physical assistance, reduce the amount of help that you provide. Here is the progression of assistance:

1. Full physical (hand-over-hand) assistance.

2. Partial physical assistance such as a tap to the arm or hand as a "reminder" to sign.

3. Gesturing and demonstrating.

4. Labeling the desired item.

5. Presenting the desired item.

After your child has mastered three to five signs, or when you feel that your child is ready, start encouraging him to produce a sound with the sign.

Language-Development Opportunities

Ideally, you want to maximize your child's opportunities to request the desired item or activity. For example, a child is more likely to learn the sign for *ball* if he is taught to sign for it 50 times a day instead of three times a day.

Here are some examples of how to incorporate this language-development tip throughout your day. For each activity, continue until your child loses interest, and be sure to follow the **Techniques to Teaching a Sign.**

Balls

- Sit with your child between your legs. Have someone sit across from you and roll a ball to your child. Have your child roll the ball back. Begin the procedures for **Techniques to Teaching a Sign.**

- Purchase a package of small Koosh™ balls from a party supply store. Cut a small hole in an inexpensive lidded cup or container that is slightly smaller than the balls. Have your child request one ball at a time to push through the hole into the cup.

- Throw a ball into a hoop, basket, or box, having your child request the ball before each toss.

Books

Have your child sign *book* before turning the page.

Snacks and Drinks

- Have your child sign each time he wants another piece or spoonful of food. For example, break or cut chips, cookies, pretzels, apples, and crackers into tiny pieces. Provide ice cream, pudding, and cereal one spoonful at a time.

- For drinks, place only 2-3 sips of the drink in the cup at a time. If your child is drinking from an open cup, make the activity more motivating by placing the drink in a child's teacup or a three-ounce disposable cup.

- Have a tea party or picnic as a variation to snack time.

Animals/Balls/Blocks/Cars/Trains

Fill a clear bag or bin with the desired object. Allow your child to remove only one item at a time after he requests it.

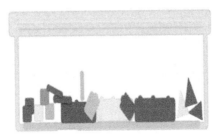

Motor Activities

Most children love activities that involve movement, which makes them great for teaching signs.

- Jumping: Help your child jump up and down to the count of five and then toss him onto the bed.

- Bounce: Bounce your child on your knee or on an exercise ball to a favorite song.

- Swing: Push your child on a swing at the playground to a count of five or a favorite song.

- Tumble: Most toddlers are unable to tumble independently. Start your child out with an assisted tumble and look for clues that your child wants to do it again.

Music/TV/Movie

Illustration of sign for *movie*

Turn on music or the TV. After your child is engaged, turn it off. She will most likely react in some way. Be playful by saying something such as, *"Uh Oh! What happened?"* When you and your child are sharing the same point of attention and your child appears to be looking for the activity to resume, ask, *"What do you want?"* and follow the **Techniques to Teaching a Sign.**

Tip 4: Be Silly

No man is exempt from saying silly things; the mischief is to say them deliberately. — Michel de Montaigne

Truly listening to spoken language is an important step in the development of speech. Create situations that encourage your child to focus more carefully on what you are saying in order to promote your child's listening skills. For example, most children love silliness and fun. (See Advisory) So, you can promote language development by letting your child catch you making an obvious mistake. For example, change the last word when singing a favorite song (*Twinkle, twinkle little bus!*).

So, tip number four is this: Incorporate silliness into everyday situations in order to promote listening skills.

Example

Abigail's mother is dressing her daughter to go outside. She puts on only one shoe and waits for Abigail to react. When she has her daughter's attention, she exclaims "*Uh oh! Mommy forgot your other _____!*" (See **Tip 7: The Cow Says Moo**).

If Abigail did not respond to her mother's silliness, her mother could have prompted her in one of these ways:

- Making a gesture by pointing to or touching the shoe.

- Making a sound (*sh*).

- Signing shoe.

- Providing a choice such as "Something is missing! Is it a hat or a shoe?"

Encourage any attempt at communication, no matter how slight.

Tip Guidelines

Before you begin, here are some guidelines to follow when using this tip to encourage speech.

- Pause after you have done something silly.

- Encourage your child to respond if he does not respond independently. For example:

    - Demonstrate a response.

    - Provide choices.

    - Make a fill-in-the-blank statement.

    - Ask a question.

    - Give a verbal hint such as an initial sound.

    - Gesture or point to your error.

    - Reinforce your child's response, even if it is just a confused look!

Language-Development Opportunities

Here are some examples of how to incorporate this language-development tip throughout your day.

Dressing and Grooming

- Put diapers on over pants.

- Put on two pairs of pants or two shirts.

- Put socks on over shoes.

- Pretend to put your child's clothing on yourself.

- Put only one sock and shoe on your child.

- Put two bottoms and no top on your child.

- Hand your child two obviously different shoes to put on.

- Pretend you are brushing your teeth with a hairbrush.

- Pretend you are brushing your hair with a toothbrush.

Story Time

- Close your eyes while "reading."

- Replace a familiar word with an incorrect word, such as *"The duck says meow."*

- Read a book upside down.

- Move your lips as if you are reading, but do not actually say anything.

- Give the book to your child to read to you.

Songs and Rhymes

- Replace a familiar word or phrase with an incorrect word or phrase such as the *"Itsy bitsy French fry went up the water spout,"* or *"This little piggy cried beep, beep, beep, all the way home."*

- Sing nonsense songs

Playtime

- Push a car and make an animal sound.

- Make an animal walk across the floor and say *"Beep, beep."*

- Pretend to put pieces from a familiar puzzle into the puzzle board from a different familiar puzzle.

Meals and Snacks

- "Forget" to give your child a spoon for food that requires one (for example, ice cream, pudding, and yogurt)

- Give your child a cup, but "forget" to fill it with juice.

- Set plates and cups on the table upside down.

Bath Time

- Put your child into a bathtub with no water.

- Put your child into an empty bathtub fully clothed.

- Use a cotton ball with soap instead of a washcloth or sponge.

Body Parts

- Touch a body part such as a nose and call it something other than what it is.

Functions/Associations

Make obviously silly statements about familiar routines, activities, animals, or objects:

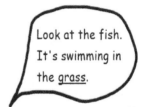

Look at the fish. It's swimming in the grass.

- Look at the bird. It's flying in the <u>water</u>.

- It's time to wash our hands. Let's turn on the <u>sand</u>.

- Yeah! You did it! Clap your <u>feet</u>.

- It's time to read. Let's pick a <u>block</u>.

- Are you thirsty? Mommy will get you a <u>phone</u>.

- Let's color. I'll get some paper and <u>soap</u>.

Anytime!

- Use the TV remote for something other than its purpose, such as a garage door opener, can opener, or key.

- Point the TV remote control at a blank wall, a picture, or a piece of furniture and pretend that you are turning on the TV.

- Put a blanket over the TV and pretend to watch it.

- Rearrange some furniture and wait for your child to comment.

- Put shaving cream on your face and "forget" to wipe it off.

- Put stickers on your face and wait for your child to comment.

- Move about the house in an unusual way, such as crawling, hopping, or walking backward.

- Pretend that you are staring at something on the ceiling.

- When cleaning up your child's toys, put them in silly places such as the refrigerator, the bathtub, or the ceiling fan.

- Sweep with the broom upside down.

- Put your child's shoes on a favorite teddy bear.

Tip 5: Talk It Out!

We are cups, constantly and quietly being filled. The trick is, knowing how to tip ourselves over and let the beautiful stuff out. — *Ray Bradbury*

Modeling means verbalizing, or *labeling*, your own actions or your child's actions. You can easily incorporate this into daily routines such as meal preparation, playtime, bath time, and bedtime.

So, tip number five is this: Verbalize your own actions (self-talk) or those of your child (parallel-talk) in order to expose your child to different aspects of language, speech, and communication. Aspects include articulation, fluency, voice and resonance, syntax, semantics, and pragmatics.

Examples

Self-Talk

Matthew's father is taking his son to the park. He is using this opportunity to promote Matthew's language development. "We are *going to the park. Should we walk or drive? I think we will walk. Daddy's putting on his blue hat and Matthew's putting on his Elmo hat. Now we will both be warm when we go outside. Let's make sure we close the door behind us.*"

Amanda is playing with her dolls and her mother is modeling language to encourage imitation. *"The baby is crying. She must be hungry. I think she would like some tasty cereal. Uh oh! We had better make sure it's not too hot. Mmmm. It tastes just right. It's delicious."*

Parallel-Talk

At bedtime, Maxine's mother describes her daughter's actions: "You are *putting on your favorite pajamas. Now you are climbing into your soft, cozy bed. Night night."*

Tip Guidelines

Before you begin, here are some guidelines to follow when using this tip to encourage speech.

- Consider your child's developmental level. Simple words, sentences, and phrases are appropriate for younger or developmentally delayed children. Sentences that are more complex are better suited for children who already have a growing vocabulary. Here are some examples.

- If your child's speech consists of single words such as mama, dada, and up, then keep labeling simple and succinct. For example, when opening a door, use words such as door, open, and out.

- If your child is beginning to put multiple words together, try labeling as complex as "Mommy is opening the front door to go outside."

- If your child falls between the previous two examples, then try the following labeling variations: open door, front door, goes out, Mommy open door, or Mommy go out.

- Adjust your labeling according to your child's language skills, gradually increasing the complexity of your sentences, or, conversely, simplifying your language.

- If your child shows interest, then spontaneously label objects. For example, if your child reaches for a stick on the playground, then tell your child that it is a stick. Your child is more likely to attempt to imitate the words for objects in which he is interested.

- Look directly at your child when you are speaking to him so that he can see your mouth movement. This also lets you know whether he is being attentive.

- Vary the types of words that you use. For example, take the time to focus explicitly on location, time, and directional words, as well as adjectives, actions, feelings, pronouns, or words that question.

Language-Development Opportunities

Here are some examples of words that you can use to incorporate this language-development tip throughout your day.

Feelings

Sad	Happy	Mad
Angry	Confused	Scared
Silly	Hungry	Cold
Thirsty	Sleepy	Tired

Variations

In addition to labeling your actions and your child's actions, consider these variations:

Other People

- Family members
- Friends
- Mail carrier
- Bus driver
- Doctor
- Landscaper
- Grocer
- Banker

Pets and Wildlife

Media

- Videos/DVDs
- Video games
- Movies
- Television
- Pictures
- Photographs
- Magazines
- Books
- Photo albums
- Posters
- Cereal boxes
- Toy packaging
- Newspaper
- Circulars
- Catalogs

Location, Time, and Directions

Behind	Under	On
Near	Over	In back of
Next to	In front of	Up
Down	Off	Outside
Inside	Upstairs	Downstairs
Soon	First	Last
Yesterday	Later	Tomorrow

Let's put your toys under your bed.

Pronouns

I	Mine	Yours
Him	His	Ours
We	Me	Us
They	Theirs	These
She	He	Her

Actions

Jump	Walk	Talk
March	Eat	Drink
Crawl	Hop	Skip
Dance	Shake	Bounce
Roll	Tumble	Clap
Touch	Point	Color
Draw	Squeeze	Pull
Push	Sit	Stand
Give	Pick up	Let go
Put down	Close	Open
Chew	Swallow	Sip
Kiss	Hug	Blow
Clean	Sleep	Climb
Swing	Slide	Paint
Build	Stack	Cut
Pour		

Words That Question

Who	What	Where
When	Why	How

Adjectives

Little	Small	Big
Large	Tall	Short
Hot	Cold	Warm
Wet	Dry	Tasty
Salty	Sweet	Sour
Spicy	Crunchy	Soft
Smooth	Hard	Bumpy
Slimy	Rough	Furry
Silky	*Colors*	*Shapes*
Fast	Fuzzy	Slow
Quick	Noisy	Quiet
Loud		

This baby chick is so fuzzy.

Tip 6: Keep It Moving!

The mother's heart is the child's schoolroom. — H. W. Beecher

Oral motor exercises have several benefits:

- They can strengthen, stretch, and coordinate mouth and facial muscles. All of which are crucial for speech production.

- They can help develop age-appropriate, functional skills such as cleaning food from a spoon, drinking from a straw or an open cup, and blowing.

- Many children find the activities fun, which encourages them to use their words in order to ask for more activities.

So, tip number six is this: Use oral motor exercises in order to help your child practice the mouth movements that are vital for speech.

Examples

Encouraging Word Formation

Dana loves to sing Old MacDonald with her mom, but she has trouble making the "*o*" sound, and "*moo*" comes out as "*muh*." Her mother has had success in helping Dana form words by incorporating oral motor strategies into Dana's daily routine. Some of the effective exercises are blowing party favors, blowing kisses, blowing bubbles, and giving Dana milk shakes with fat straws. These exercises help Dana learn to round and strengthen her lips.

Encouraging Word Clarity

Joey has a good vocabulary for his age, but his family has difficulty understanding what he says. His father has recently added oral motor strategies into Joey's daily routines. The goal is to help Joey pronounce his words more clearly. Some of the activities include using a vibrating toothbrush, daily squirts of sour candy, and oral motor songs.

Tip Guidelines

Before you begin, here are some guidelines to follow when using this tip to encourage speech.

- Straws, cups, whistles, and other devices are tools and you must control the tools at all times.

- Don't permit biting the tool unless the activity calls for it.

- Place your child in a physically stable position. For example, seat him with a straight back and feet flat on the floor (hips, knees, and ankles at a 90-degree angle). You also can position him prone, with elbows under his shoulders and his head up and forward.

Lip, Tongue, and Cheek Exercises

Practice lip, tongue, and cheek exercises either while sitting across from your child or while sitting behind your child facing a mirror. Demonstrate the exercise and then encourage your child to imitate you.

Lip Exercises

Lip exercises can help improve all of these skills.

- Jaw stability, which helps with drinking from an open cup.

- Lip closure, which helps with blowing, sucking, and stripping solids from a spoon or fork.

- Lip strength, which helps with sucking and drinking with a straw.

- Tongue retraction and protrusion.

- Puckering and lip rounding, which helps improve breadth support and control of airflow.

Here are some examples:

- Hold licorice (Twizzlers™ are a great motivator), a stick, or stir straw between the lips.

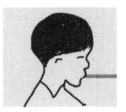

- Say *oo-ee, oo-ee* with exaggerated lip movements and encourage imitation.

- Hum and encourage imitation.

- Exaggerate a smile (without showing your teeth) and then straighten the lips. Repeat.

- Suck pudding, applesauce, or thickened liquids with straws of varying widths and shapes, progressing from easiest to hardest.

- Apply a type of lip balm to your child's lips or brush his lips with different textures, such as a toothbrush, warm, dry, or cool washcloth, tongue depressor, or spoon.

Tongue Exercises

Tongue exercises can help improve all of these skills:

- Protrusion and retraction.

- Lateralization (side-to-side movement).

- Movement of food inside the mouth.

Here are some examples:

- Lick a favorite thick food, such as pudding, frosting, or ice cream, off a spoon or stick.

- Push a spoon or stick away from the mouth using your tongue.

- Make raspberries.

- Blow instruments (horns, whistles, flutes, recorders, sirens, harmonicas).

- Say *blah, blah, blah.*

- Spread food on the lips and then lick it off.

- Place syrup on the outside corners of the mouth and demonstrate how to lick it off.

- Place a favorite food, such as syrup, pudding, sauce, ice cream, or cake frosting, in a very small cup and use the tongue to lick it off the bottom.

- Using the tongue, hold a piece of cereal or other small snack behind the top front teeth.

- Lick a favorite thick food off a plate.

- Follow a lollipop from one corner of the outside of the mouth to the next with the tongue.

Cheek Exercises

Cheek exercises can help improve the following skills:

- Strength and flexibility.

- Tongue lateralization.

- Blowing.

Here are some examples:

- Fill the cheeks with air and then "pop" them.

- Place tiny pieces of paper (prepackaged confetti or "hole-punch" scraps are great) in a cup or jar and blow them with or without a straw.

- Suck in the cheeks, making a "fish face."

- Blow bubbles using various types of bubble wands.

- Blow instruments (horns, whistles, flutes, recorders, sirens, harmonicas).

- Race cotton or pom-pom balls or lightweight plastic toys across a table.

- Blow a pinwheel.

- Make bubbles in a cup of milk by blowing through a straw.

- Make works of art with blow pens.

Intra-oral Stimulation Exercises

Tools and Resources to Stimulate the Oral Mechanisms

Note: Stimulate both sides of the mouth consistently.

- "Tasty" applications (for example, sour candy spray, lemon, vinegar, soy sauce, garlic, curry). You can add these products to food to increase awareness or apply them to your child's mouth by hand, on a spoon, or by spray.

- Toothbrush or vibrating toothbrush. Singing a short song or counting might help distract an unsure child.

- Cold applications (ice pops, cold washcloth) to stimulate the inside of the cheeks, gums, palate, and tongue.

- The Jiggler™ is a facial and oral massager that uses low-intensity vibration to stimulate the oral mechanism.

- Z-Vibe™ can be purchased with a variety of tips, including a spoon. It uses extremely low-intensity vibration to stimulate the gums, palate, and tongue. You can also use this tool on the cheeks and lips.

Z-Vibe

- Vibrating teethers vibrate when firm pressure is applied. You can purchase them in most stores that sell infant teethers.

Chewy Tube

- Chewy Tubes™ enable a child to safely practice chewing and biting skills. They might also be useful in redirecting inappropriate chewing.

Oral Motor Songs

Most children love repetition, music, and silly faces. Oral motor songs are a fun way to incorporate all of these components into speech therapy. Oral motor songs encourage your child to use their lips, cheeks, and tongue.

Note: You can make up your own songs or rhymes, or you can use the examples located in **Appendix 3: Oral Motor Songs**.

These exercises are a great warm-up to mealtime or a structured language activity. Here are the steps:

1. Sit cross from your child or sit behind your child facing a mirror.

2. Sing the song (*Twinkle, Twinkle, Little* Star is a good tune to follow), or read the rhyme.

3. Demonstrate the movement of your lips.

4. Encourage your child to imitate each movement three to 10 times.

5. Reinforce any attempt at imitation, no matter how slight.

Tip 7: The Cow Says Moo

The most precious things in speech are the pauses. — Sir Ralph Richardson

Sometimes toddlers develop scattered language skills. As a quick test, show your child a cookie and ask him what it is.

- If he can easily tell you what it is, then he likely has good word-retrieval skills.

- If he knows it is a cookie, and he has said *cookie* in the past, but he cannot tell you now that is a cookie, then he might have poor word-retrieval skills

Now tell your child that it is a cookie and ask him to say *cookie.*

- If he easily repeats the word, then he likely has good verbal-planning and on-demand imitation skills.

- If your child struggles to repeat the word *cookie,* but he can spontaneously say *cookie* throughout the day, then he likely has poor verbal-planning skills. Toddlers with poor planning skills find it difficult to repeat a word on demand.

To help your child improve his word-retrieval and verbal-planning skills, you can use a technique called "intraverbals."[1] *Intraverbals* is the behavioral psychologist's term for giving your child a jump-start on repeating the target word while relieving him of the pressure to say the word on his own. You can turn any phrase or common expression into an intraverbal.

Intraverbals fall into two categories:

- Fill-in-the-blanks (*"The cow says ____."*)

- Questions (*"What does the cow say?"*)

Both methods are effective in addressing word-retrieval and verbal-planning skills.

So, tip number seven is this: Help your child find the right word.

Examples

Practicing Planning (Imitating the target word)

Johnny's mother is helping him build his word-retrieval and verbal-planning skills with animal sounds. She starts by making the statement *"The cow says moo."* She then

---

[1] The intraverbal technique was proposed by behavioral psychologist B. F. Skinner.

repeats the statement again, leaving out the last word, *"The cow says _____."* She pauses and waits for Johnny to fill in the blank. Johnny responds correctly with *"moo,"* and his mother then reinforces his response by repeating it back to him, *"Yes! The cow says moo!"* If Johnny could not remember the word *"moo,"* his mother would have told him the word and then continued to practice.

Practicing Retrieval (Remembering the right word)

Chrissy's father is also helping his daughter address her word-retrieval and verbal-planning skills with animal sounds. He starts by asking Chrissy, *"What does the cow say?"* and then he pauses and waits for her response. Chrissy responds by saying *"moo."* Her father reinforces her response by repeating it back to her, *"Yes! The cow says moo!"* If Chrissy could not answer her father's question, her father would have told her the answer and then continued to practice.

Tip Guidelines

Before you begin, here are some guidelines to follow when using this tip to encourage speech:

- Pause three to five seconds after each statement or question to give your child time to respond.

- Reinforce your child's response by repeating it back to him. *"Yes! The cow says moo."*

- Switch the order of your statements or questions. If you have already said, *"The cow says _____,"* then the next time say, *"Moo says the _____."*

- Start with one or two phrases, animal sounds, and familiar songs or rhymes that your child uses throughout the day.

Language-Development Opportunities

Here are some examples of how to incorporate this language-development tip throughout your day.

Phrases and More (fill in the blank)

- Ready, set, <u>go</u>

- Have a nice <u>day</u>

- Thank <u>you.</u>

- I love <u>you.</u>

- Good <u>night.</u>

- I <u>did it.</u>

- Up and <u>down.</u>

- One, two, <u>three.</u>

- The <u>end.</u>

Animal Sounds

Fill in the blank	Question
Cow says <u>moo</u>	What does the cow say?
Cat says <u>meow</u>	What does the cat say?
Pig says <u>oink</u>	What does the pig say?
Sheep says <u>baa</u>	What does the sheep say?
Horse says <u>neigh</u>	What does the horse say?
Duck says <u>quack</u>	What does the duck say?
Dog says <u>woof</u>	What does the dog say?

Pretend Play

Fill in the blank	Question
Car goes <u>beep-beep</u>	What sound does the car make?
Train goes <u>woo-woo</u>	What sound does the train make?
Baby goes <u>wah</u>	What sound does the baby make?

Plane goes <u>woosh</u>	What sound does the plane make?

Actions (fill in the blank)

- Clap your <u>hands</u>.

- Turn the <u>page</u>.

- Open the <u>door</u>.

- Close the <u>door</u>.

- Stomp your <u>feet</u>.

- Sit <u>down</u>.

- Stand <u>up</u>.

Color and Object Functions and Associations

Fill in the blank	Question
A hat goes on your <u>head</u>.	Where does your hat go?
Shoes go on your <u>feet</u>.	Where do your shoes go?
You wash your hands with <u>soap</u>.	What do you wash your hands with?
The grass is <u>green</u>.	What color is the grass?
The sun is <u>yellow</u>.	What color is the sun?
The sky is <u>blue</u>.	What color is the sky?

Body Part Functions

Fill in the blank	Question
You see with your <u>eyes</u>.	What do you see with?
You chew with your <u>mouth</u>.	What do you chew with?
You smile with your <u>mouth</u>.	What do you smile with?
You speak with your <u>mouth</u>.	What do you speak with?

You smell with your <u>nose</u>.	What do you smell with?
You march with your <u>legs</u>.	What do you march with?
You hear with your <u>ears</u>.	What do you hear with?
You clap with your <u>hands</u>.	What do you clap with?
You stomp with your <u>feet</u>.	What do you stomp with?

Songs and Nursery Rhymes

Use the songs and rhymes in **Appendix 1 (Children's Songs and Nursery Rhymes)** to work on letters, sounds and words. Here are some suggestions:

- Twinkle twinkle little <u>star</u>

- The itsy bitsy spider went <u>up</u>

- E-I-E-I-<u>O</u>

- Row, row, row your <u>boat</u>

- Baa baa black <u>sheep</u>

- One, two buckle my <u>shoe</u>

Tip 8: Break It Down

If you procrastinate when faced with a big difficult problem...break the problem into parts, and handle one part at a time. — *Robert Collier*

Your child has a few words. He makes his needs known to you. He answers your questions in short sentences. He happily holds meaningful conversations with family and friends.

The problem is that no one can understand what he is saying.

Although articulation is not the primary concern when it comes to toddler speech development, unintelligibility can significantly affect play skills and social-emotional development. This situation creates frustration for both parents and children, and leads to inappropriate behaviors such as lengthy tantrums and aggression.

So, tip number eight is this: Break words down into smaller components in order to help your child communicate more effectively.

Understanding Sound Development

Here is an overview of the progression of sound development.

- Typically, the first consonant sounds children make are called *bilabials*. These sounds, *b*, *m* and *p*, require the use of both lips. Other early sounds that might be heard during play and feeding include *d* and *t*.

- Children generally begin saying *mama* or *dada* non-specifically between 6.5 and 11 months of age. They begin saying *mama* or *dada* specifically between 11 and 14 months of age.

- At around eight to 12 months of age, children begin to produce single consonant-vowel combinations such as *da* and *ba*.

- In a typically developing progression, the next consonants that children babble include *n*, *g*, *k*, *w*, *h*, *f*, *v*, *th*, *s*, *z*, *l*, and *r* (12 -15 months).

- Generally, the specific age range in which children clearly produce sounds varies. However, most experts include *k*, *g*, *f*, *v*, *sh*, *ch*, *s*, *z*, *l*, *th*, and *r* among the later sounds (three to eight years of age).

Example

Thirty-month old Tom has about 20 words but his parents are concerned because his speech does not seem to be progressing. They are also concerned because when he tries to speak in sentences, no one can understand what he is saying.

Both Tom and his parents are becoming frustrated. Tom's parents put together a list of the sounds that Tom can make. They use this list to figure out what sounds Tom can and cannot produce.

From this list, they learn that Tom has a problem with consonant sounds. So, his parents make up a speech bin for consonant sounds. Tom's parents hope that by breaking words down into smaller components, Tom will be able to eventually enunciate more clearly, increase his vocabulary, and be more easily understood.

Tip Guidelines

Before you begin, here are some guidelines to follow when using this tip to encourage speech:

- If your child is not vocalizing at all, prompt your child for simple sounds, not three-syllable words. It is crucial for your child to feel successful, even if that success is in the attempt itself.

- Create a *speech bin* to include objects or pictures representing the target sounds. Using the same pictures or objects helps your child become familiar with them. At the same time, you always have the necessary tools available for use.

- When introducing this activity to your child, you can take one object from the bin at a time, or you can present your child with a choice of two objects.

- If your child does not attempt to vocalize, bring the target object near your mouth and over-enunciate the target sound or word.

- Praise each attempt, keeping in mind that the goal, as always, is not to frustrate your child.

Language-Development Opportunities

Here are some examples of how to incorporate this language-development tip throughout your day.

A Speech Bin for Initial Sounds

Here are some examples of what to include in a speech bin to encourage initial sounds.

- Pie for /*p*/

- Lion/tiger for /*rrr*/

- Dog for /*d*/

- Fish for /*f*/

- Nose (from Mr. Potato Head™) for /*n*/

- Cup for *guh-guh-guh* (as if you are drinking from a cup)

- Snake for /*s*/

- Teeth (from Mr. Potato Head™) for /*t*/

- Apple for *a*

- Ape for *ay*

- Fake food (to represent *eat*) for *ee*

- Elephant for *eh*

- Eye (from Mr. Potato Head™) to represent *igh*

- Picture of Mommy for /*m*/

- Ball for /*b*/

- Cat for /*k*/

- Sun cutout to represent hot /*h*/

A Speech Bin for Simple Consonant-Vowel Words

For children who are able to produce most age-appropriate sounds in isolation but struggle with blending sounds, start with a speech bin that contains objects and pictures to represent simple consonant-vowel words. You can easily expand your target words by creating a list of consonant-vowel words and then finding child-friendly objects or pictures to represent them.

Tip: If your child has difficulty following through with the entire word, have him imitate one sound or syllable at a time (/b/-/ee/). As with all techniques, start out by providing your child with the most support that he needs in order to succeed. Gradually reduce the amount of support that you provide.

Here are some examples of what to include in a speech bin to encourage consonant-vowel words.

- Bee

- Money for *pay*

- Ribbon for *bow*

- Slime for *goo*

- Stingray toy for *ray*

- Hay

- Key

- Owl for *hoo*

- Baby for *coo*

- Mirror *me*

A Speech Bin for More Advanced Sound Combinations

After you and your child are ready to move beyond initial and simple consonant-vowel words, expand your speech bin to include other types of sound combinations.

Tip: Clap or tap to two or more syllable words. For more ways in which to pair sound with movement, refer to **Tip 9: Get Your Groove On**.

Here are some examples of what to include in a speech bin to encourage sound combinations:

- Consonant-vowel-consonant such as cat, dog, man

- Consonant-vowel-consonant-vowel such as puppy (*pu-pee*), kitty (*kih-tee*), Nemo (*nee-moh*)

- Vowel-consonant such as oak, eat, ape

- Vowel-consonant-vowel such as Abby (*aaa-bee*), okay (*oh-kay*), emu (*ee-meeoo*)

Tip 9: Get Your Groove On

Nothing happens until something moves. –Albert Einstein

Movement and rhythm can stimulate the neural pathways that link the various parts of the brain, including the frontal lobes. The frontal lobes play an important role in the development of such abilities as facial movement, language production, problem solving, planning, working memory, and motor function.

Moreover, rhythmical movement might aid in organizing information received through the senses. When information is better organized, it is more likely to aid language development.

So, tip number nine is this: Pair movement with sound in order to help your child learn language through a sensation other than sound.

Examples

Encouraging the Quiet Child

Dawn is twenty-one months old. Her parents are concerned because she is very quiet. She does not have any words other than *Mama* and *Dada*. In addition, Dawn is a sedentary child. She prefers to sit quietly and look through pictures in a book. Dawn's parents are going to try pairing movement with sound to encourage Dawn to be more vocal.

Because Dawn likes music, her parents teach her to sing the alphabet song while waving a ribbon scarf. With her mother's help, Dawn slowly moves the ribbon scarf in different directions to the beat of the song. When her mother sings "*a*," they lift the ribbon up. When her mother sings "*b*," they swing the ribbon back down, and so on. Dawn's parents also encourage her to bang on objects to the beat of favorite songs. They use objects such as pots, a tambourine, and a drum.

Encouraging the Unfocused Child

At twenty-one-months-old, Frankie is the opposite of Dawn. He is always on the go. His parents are concerned about his limited speech, but they have trouble getting him to sit down and focus. They decide to include guided movement activities to help him organize the information that he is receiving from his senses, as well as motivate him to focus on speech exercises.

Because Frankie loves to jump, his parents help him jump on an exercise ball to the beat of *Five Little Monkeys*. They pause periodically throughout the song and encourage

Frankie to fill in a word (**Tip 7: The Cow Says Moo**). Because Frankie wants to continue jumping, he is motivated to try to say the target word.

As another daily strategy, Frankie's parents place a collapsible tunnel on a supported incline. Each time Frankie crawls up the tunnel, his parents say, "*up, up, up.*" Each time he climbs down the tunnel, they say, "*down, down, down.*" Eventually, Frankie begins to use these words himself during the activity and throughout the day.

Encouraging Articulation

At thirty-two months old, Louie has a large vocabulary, but he is not easily understood. Three-syllable words and often three-word sentences are difficult for him. *Bumble Bee* sounds like "*bu-bee.*" "*I want juice*" sounds like "*wa oose.*"

Because Louie loves blocks, his parents decide to use blocks as a "speech tool" to help Louie count the sounds in words and in simple sentences. For example, for three-syllable words such as *bum-ble-bee*, Louie's parents have him stack three blocks, one at a time. Each block corresponds to a sound. The blocks serve as a visual cue (three blocks = three sounds. They also help Louie to "feel" the sounds (three stacking movements = three sounds).

Louie's parents also use the bouncing a ball as a strategy. "*I want juice*" is three bounces. In this case, each bounce corresponds to a one-syllable word.

Language-Development Opportunities

Here are some examples of how to incorporate this language-development tip throughout your day.

Me and My Body

- Slowly tap or clap out sounds and words to help your child better hear how the syllables are broken down. For example, *da-da*, *mom-my* and *uh-oh* are two taps/claps, while *but-ter-fly*, *I did it*, and *I love you* are three taps/claps.

- Sit across from or behind your child, and either tap out the sounds on the table or tap them gently on his body (leg, arm, shoulder, back). Some children, especially those with good imitation skills, might easily be able to imitate the proper number of taps/claps without any physical prompting. Others might require hand-over-hand assistance.

- Clap, tap, or bounce your child on your knee or lap to the beat of a song or rhyme, one bounce for each syllable. For example, *twin-kle, twin-kle lit-tle star* uses seven bounces. Stop the movement briefly at natural pauses and give him an opportunity to vocalize that he wants you to continue. Young children especially enjoy the movement shift associated with such bouncing rhymes as *Trot Trot to Boston.* They listen attentively for that much-anticipated moment when they get to fall back (*look out you don't fall in!*).

- As an alternative to bouncing, tapping or clapping to the beat of a song or rhyme, try marching, jumping, or stomping your feet instead.

- Give your child a piggy back ride, play horse, or sway or bounce him to the presentation of sound (for example, whistle, tongue clicks, hum, sing). Then stop the sound and movement simultaneously. This technique increases awareness of the presence or absence of sound. As a result, he might vocalize that he wants you to do it again.

- Play sound-movement imitation games. Make a movement, such as two claps, to a sound, and encourage your child to imitate. Alternate the number of sounds (that is, one clap versus three claps) as well as the pace (faster or slower).

- Sing traditional songs such as *Itsy Bitsy Spider*, and help your child follow the movements.

Toys and Stuff

Pair sounds with movement while using toys or other items lying around the house. Refer to the examples earlier in this chapter (**Encouraging the Quiet Child** and **Encouraging Articulation**). You can turn nearly any toy or object around the house into an effective "speech tool." The amount of physical prompting or support depends on your child's skill level.

- Stack blocks.

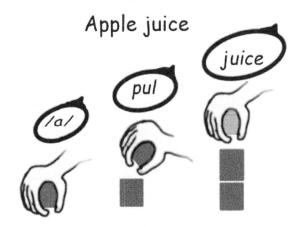

- Put balls or other objects into a cup or container.

- Bang on a drum or pot.

- Bounce a ball.

- Swing a ribbon scarf.

- Bang a tambourine.

- Bang together blocks or spoons.

- Shake a noisemaker.

- Shake pom-poms.

- Color to sound (*dot-dot-dot, up and down, back and forth, round and round*).

- Place a collapsible child's tunnel on an incline (floor to couch for example). Stuff pillows under the tunnel for support. Have your child climb up and down the tunnel. Use this as motivation to imitate a sound. Label his movements to encourage imitation (*Up, up, up! Down, down, down! Weeeee!*).

- Bounce your child on an exercise ball to a favorite song. If your child is not yet ready to balance himself on the ball, hold him on your lap and bounce with him. If your child wants to sit on the ball by himself, you can steady the ball by placing one side against a couch or wall and holding your child at his hips. As another alternative, you can kneel or sit behind the ball and press down on your child's shoulders while bouncing him on the ball. Some children find this deep input very soothing.

Rhythmical Movement

Any type of rhythmical movement can help stimulate language. Try some of these ideas:

- Give your child a small stick with which to conduct music. Demonstrate the activity for your child if he is unsure of what to do.

- Lead a parade or marching band. Give your child a baton and encourage him to march to his favorite music. This is a great group activity.

- Play and sing *Ring Around the Rosie*.

- Provide your child with a different type of sensation by allowing him to play with finger paints or whip cream on a cookie sheet. Sing *Wheels on the Bus* and help him go *up* and *down* or *swish, swish, swish* with the paint or whip cream.

- Swing your child on a scooter board to songs or counting. Sturdy boxes and laundry baskets can be used as alternatives to scooters.

- Shake, raise, and lower a parachute to music. Place lightweight balls or toys on top of the parachute and pop them off. This is another great group activity.

Tip 10: Books, Books, and More Books

There is no substitute for books in the life of a child. - *Mary Ellen Chase*

Books play a key role in language development by:

- Exposing children to different aspects of speech, language, and communication.

- Introducing children to concepts, topics, and places to which they might not otherwise be exposed.

- Helping children relax and wind down.

- Motivating children to move and groove.

- Presenting an opportunity for you to bond with your child.

So, tip number 10 is this: Incorporate books into your strategy for encouraging language development.

Note: Children learn by having fun. If your child does not like books, then you must be persistent in order to succeed with this tip.

How to Choose a Book

For very young children or those who are always too busy to sit for story time, look for books that fall into these four categories:

- Song books

- Books with moving parts (turn wheel, pop-up, and flap books)

- Sensory/touch and feel books

- Books that include a child's favorite character

When your child is ready to sit for story time and attend to the words as well as the pictures, introduce these other favorites:

- Interactive electronic books

- Books that encourage motor movement (Eric Carle's *From Head to Toe* is one of my favorites)

- Individualized books made up of pictures representing words that a child is able to verbalize, even if articulation is not exact. These personalized books can be easily made by pasting photographs and pictures from magazines or circulars onto paper, or by placing them into an inexpensive photo album.

Examples

Learning How to Take Control

Duncan will not sit still for a book. He only looks at a page or two before climbing off his mother's lap to find something else to do. In addition, he battles with his mother for control of the book. If his mother allows him to hold the book, he just flips through quickly, and he does not let his mother read to him.

Frustrated, Duncan's parents decide to change their strategy. First, they borrow some simple peek-a-boo books from the library. Next, they maintain control by holding the book, but they allow Duncan to open the flaps.

This strategy is effective for Duncan. He enjoys discovering what is hidden behind each flap. In addition, opening the flaps gives him a sense of control. Now that Duncan sits still for books for short periods, his parents can expand on this new interest.

Making Books Part of the Development Plan

Billy is diagnosed with autism. At nearly three years old, his speech is limited to only a few sounds. He loves books and his parents take advantage of this by reading to him at every opportunity. They incorporate many of the strategies outlined in this book to promote Billy's speech development.

Even though Billy still struggles to speak, his parents are happy that he is able to request a book with sign language, use simple signs to label many of the pictures in his favorite books, and fill in some familiar sounds.

Tip Guidelines

Before you begin, here are some guidelines to follow when using this tip to encourage speech:

- Adults hold the book. By holding the book, you remain in charge of the activity, and you can set the pace. Your child also does not have an opportunity to flip pages without attending to the words.

- Create a positive atmosphere. Read books when your child is not distracted by other activities such as television. Establishing a routine is also a good idea. Just before or after a nap, bath, or bedtime is a great starting point for all books except for motor/movement books.

- Put on a show. Sing the words instead of reading them, vary your tone, pitch, and assign different voices to different characters. If you are animated, then your child will be more interested in what you are doing.

- Be brief. You don't have to read every word on the page. In fact, you don't have to read the words at all. You can simply show a page and label one or two pictures. Start simple. Get through the activity before your child loses interest or, worse, begins to tantrum. Keep it fun!

- Lower your expectations. If the book has five pages but your child starts to fuss at page 2, then skip to the end of the book and indicate that the book is finished with a phrase such as "*All done.*" If you stop reading the moment that she fusses, you are reinforcing inappropriate behavior and encouraging her to repeat the behavior the next time you read a book to her.

Language-Development Opportunities

Once your child begins to enjoy books, incorporate some of the techniques described in the previous chapters of this book into your story time.

- If reading is part of your bedtime routine, encourage your child to request a story by using a sound, word, sentence, or a sign, depending on his skill level. (**Tip 1: Do What Does Not Come Naturally**)

- Present your child with choices between two books. Allow him to choose who reads the book and where to sit. Ask questions and let your child choose the answer. (**Tip 2: Juice or Milk?**)

- Encourage your child to request the book with the sign for *book*. (**Tip 3: Simple Signs**)

- Pretend to read the book upside down or replace familiar words with silly words. (**Tip 4: Be Silly**)

- Expand on the book by labeling what you see in the pictures. Encourage your child to do the same. (**Tip 5: Talk It Out!**)

- Ask questions about favorite stories or leave out key words. Pause to give your child an opportunity to respond. (**Tip 7: The Cow Says Moo**)

- Tap or pair some other type of movement with the words or phrases in the book. Encourage your child to do the same. (**Tip 9: Get Your Groove On**)

Appendix 1: Children's Songs and Nursery Rhymes[2]

Old MacDonald

Old MacDonald had a farm, E I E I O.
And on his farm he had some chicks, E I E I O.
With a chick chick here and a chick chick there,
here a chick, there a chick, everywhere a chick chick.
Old MacDonald had a farm, E I E I O.

Old MacDonald had a farm, E I E I O.
And on his farm he had a cow, E I E I O.
With a moo moo here and a moo moo there,
here a moo, there a moo, everywhere a moo moo.
Old MacDonald had a farm, E I E I O.

Old MacDonald had a farm, E I E I O.
And on his farm he had a pig, E I E I O.
With an oink oink here and an oink oink there,
here an oink, there an oink, everywhere an oink oink.
Old MacDonald had a farm, E I E I O.

Old MacDonald had a farm, E I E I O.
And on his farm he had some ducks, E I E I O.
With a quack quack here and a quack quack there,
here a quack, there a quack , everywhere a quack quack.
Old MacDonald had a farm, E I E I O.

Old MacDonald had a farm, E I E I O.
And on his farm he had a horse, E I E I O.
With a neigh neigh here and a neigh neigh there,
here a neigh, there a neigh, everywhere a neigh neigh.
Old MacDonald had a farm, E I E I O.

---

[2] Public Domain

Itsy Bitsy Spider

The itsy bitsy spider
climbed up the waterspout.
Down came the rain
and washed the spider out.
Out came the sun
and dried up all the rain.
So the itsy-bitsy spider
climbed up the spout again!

Ring Around the Rosie

Ring around the rosie,
a pocket full of posies;
Ashes, Ashes,
all stand still.
(Children hold still)

The King has sent his daughter,
to fetch a pail of water;
(Children hold hands and dance around in a circle)
Ashes, Ashes,
all fall down.
(Children fall to the floor)

The bird upon the steeple,
sits high above the people;
(Children hold hands and dance around in a circle)
Ashes, Ashes,
all kneel down.
(Children kneel)

The wedding bells are ringing,
the boys and girls are singing;
(Children hold hands and dance around in a circle)
Ashes, Ashes,
all fall down.
(Children fall to the floor)

Rock-a-bye Baby

Rock a bye baby, on the tree top.
When the wind blows the cradle will rock.
When the bough breaks the cradle will fall,
and down will come baby, cradle and all.

Row, Row, Row Your Boat

Row, row, row your boat
Gently down the stream.
Merrily, merrily, merrily, merrily,
Life is but a dream.

Row, row, row your boat
Gently around the lake
Merrily, merrily, merrily, merrily,
Life's a piece of cake.

Twinkle, Twinkle, Little Star

Twinkle, twinkle, little star,
how I wonder what you are!
Up above the world so high,
like a diamond in the sky.
Twinkle, twinkle, little star,
how I wonder what you are!

BINGO

There was a farmer had a dog,
And Bingo was his name-O.
B-I-N-G-O!
B-I-N-G-O!
B-I-N-G-O!
And Bingo was his name-O!

There was a farmer had a dog,
And Bingo was his name-O.
(Clap)-I-N-G-O!
(Clap)-I-N-G-O!
(Clap)-I-N-G-O!
And Bingo was his name-O!

There was a farmer had a dog,
And Bingo was his name-O!
(Clap, Clap)-N-G-O!
(Clap, Clap)-N-G-O!
(Clap-Clap)-N-G-O!
And Bingo was his name-O!

There was a farmer had a dog,
And Bingo was his name-O.
(Clap, Clap, Clap)-G-O!
(Clap, Clap, Clap)-G-O!
(Clap, Clap, Clap)-G-O!
And Bingo was his name-O!

There was a farmer had a dog,
And Bingo was his name-O.
(Clap, Clap, Clap, Clap)-O!
(Clap, Clap, Clap, Clap)-O!
(Clap, Clap, Clap, Clap)-O!
And Bingo was his name-O!

There was a farmer had a dog,
And Bingo was his name-O.
(Clap, Clap, Clap, Clap, Clap)
(Clap, Clap, Clap, Clap, Clap)
(Clap, Clap, Clap, Clap, Clap)
And Bingo was his name-O!

If You're Happy and You Know It (Traditional)

If you're happy and you know it clap your hands.

(clap clap)

If you're happy and you know it clap your hands.

(clap clap)

If you're happy and you know it, and you really want to show it, if you're happy and you know it clap your hands.

(clap clap)

Proceed with other verses that replace "clap your hands" with alternate phrases such as "shout hooray."

The Wheels on the Bus

The wheels on the bus go round and round.
Round and round.
Round and round.

The wheels on the bus go round and round,
all through the town!

The people on the bus go up and down.
Up and down.
Up and down.
The people on the bus go up and down,
all through the town!

The horn on the bus goes beep, beep, beep.
Beep, beep beep.
Beep, beep, beep.
The horn on the bus goes beep, beep, beep.
all through the town!

The wipers on the bus go swish, swish, swish.
Swish, swish, swish.
Swish, swish, swish.
The wipers on the bus go swish, swish, swish,
all through the town!

The signals on the bus go blink, blink, blink.
Blink, blink, blink.
Blink, blink, blink.
The signals on the bus go blink, blink, blink,
all through the town!

The motor on the bus goes zoom, zoom, zoom.
Zoom, zoom, zoom.
Zoom, zoom, zoom.
The motor on the bus goes zoom, zoom, zoom,
all through the town!

The babies on the bus go waa, waa, waa.
Waa, waa, waa.
Waa, waa, waa.
The babies on the bus go waa, waa, waa,
all through the town!

The parents on the bus go shh, shh, shh.
Shh, shh, shh.
Shh, shh, shh.
The parents on the bus go shh, shh, shh,
all through the town!

The mommy on the bus says, I love you.
I love you.
I love you.
The daddy on the bus says, I love you, too,
all through the town.

Head, Shoulders, Knees, and Toes

Head, shoulders, knees, and toes,
knees and toes

Head, shoulders, knees, and toes,
knees and toes

And eyes
And ears
And mouth
And nose

Head, shoulders, knees, and toes,
knees and toes

Mary Had a Little Lamb

Mary had a little lamb,
little lamb, little lamb.
Mary had a little lamb,
its fleece was white as snow.
And everywhere that Mary went,
Mary went, Mary went.
Everywhere that Mary went
the lamb was sure to go.

It followed her to school one day,
school one day, school one day.
It followed her to school one day,
which was against the rule.
It made the children laugh and play,
laugh and play, laugh and play.
It made the children laugh and play,
to see a lamb at school.

So the teacher turned him out
turned him out, turned him out.

So the teacher turned him out,
and sent him straight away.

This Little Piggie

This little piggie went to market.
This little piggie stayed home.
This little piggie had roast beef.
This little piggie had none.
And this little piggie cried, "Wee! Wee! Wee!"
All the way home.

Five Little Monkeys

5 little monkeys jumping on a bed.
One fell off and bumped his head.
Mama called the doctor and the doctor said,
"No more monkeys jumping on a bed."

4 little monkeys jumping on a bed.
One fell off and bumped his head.
Mama called the doctor and the doctor said,
"No more monkeys jumping on a bed."

3 little monkeys jumping on a bed.
One fell off and bumped his head.
Mama called the doctor and the doctor said,
"No more monkeys jumping on a bed."

2 little monkeys jumping on a bed.
One fell off and bumped his head.
Mama called the doctor and the doctor said,
"No more monkeys jumping on a bed."

1 little monkey jumping on a bed.
He fell off and bumped his head.
Mama called the doctor and the doctor said,
"No more monkeys jumping on a bed."

Five Little Ducks

5 little ducks went out one day,
over the hills and far away.
Mommy (daddy) duck called quack, quack, quack,
but only 4 little ducks came back.

4 little ducks went out one day,
over the hills and far away.
Mommy (daddy) duck called quack, quack, quack,
but only 3 little ducks came back.

3 little ducks went out one day,
over the hills and far away.
Mommy (daddy) duck called quack, quack, quack,
but only 2 little ducks came back.

2 little ducks went out one day,
over the hills and far away.
Mommy (daddy) duck called quack, quack, quack,
but only 1 little duck came back.

1 little duck went out one day,
over the hills and far away.
Mommy (daddy) duck called quack, quack, quack,
but none of the little ducks came back.

Sad mommy (daddy) duck went out one day,
over the hills and far away.
Mommy (daddy) duck called quack, quack, quack,
and all of the 5 little ducks came back.

Trot Trot to Boston

Trot, trot to Boston.
Trot, trot to Lynn.
Trot back home again.
Look out you don't fall in.

Baa, Baa Black Sheep (Mother Goose)

Baa, baa, black sheep,
have you any wool?
Yes sir, yes sir,
three bags full;

One for my master.
One for my dame.
And one for the little boy
that lives in our lane.

Hickory, Dickory, Dock (Mother Goose)

Hickory, dickory, dock.
The mouse ran up the clock.

The clock struck one.
The mouse ran down.
Hickory, dickory, dock.

Hey! Diddle, Diddle (Mother Goose)

Hey! diddle, diddle,
the cat and the fiddle,
the cow jumped over the moon.
The little dog laughed
to see such sport,
and the dish ran away with the spoon.

Jack and Jill (Mother Goose)

Jack and Jill went up the hill,
to fetch a pail of water;
Jack fell down, and broke his crown,
and Jill came tumbling after.

Little Miss Muffet (Mother Goose)

Little Miss Muffet
sat on a tuffet,
eating her curds and whey.
Along came a spider,
who sat down beside her,
and frightened Miss Muffet away.

One, Two, Buckle My Shoe (Mother Goose)

One, two,
buckle my shoe;
Three, four,
shut the door;
Five, six,
pick-up sticks;

Seven eight,
lay them straight;
Nine, ten,
a good fat hen.

Pat-a-cake, Pat-a-cake (Mother Goose)

Pat-a-cake, pat-a-cake,
baker's man,
bake me a cake

as fast as you can;
prick it and pat it,
and mark it with B,
and put it in the oven
for baby and me.

Appendix 2: Simple Signs for Toddlers

Food

Chip

Pat your left shoulder with the fingers of your right hand.

Cookie

Twist the fingertips of your right hand side to side on the palm of your left hand.

Cracker

Tap the palm of your right hand twice near the elbow of your bent left arm.

Drink

Form a *c* shape with your right hand and bring it to your mouth as if you are pretending to drink from a cup.

Activities

Movie/TV

Place the heels of your palms together and twist your right hand.

Music

Form a cradle by slightly bending your left arm at the elbow, then move your right open hand, pinky downward, back and forth over your left arm, as if you are brushing something from your arm.

Objects

Ball

Pretend you are holding a ball by placing the fingertips of your hands toward each other.

Block - See On

Book

Pretend you are opening a book by placing your palms together and then folding them open, keeping your pinkies together.

Car

Pretend you are driving by placing your fisted hands in front of you and moving them in an alternating up and down position.

Puzzle/Piece

Palm facing inward, tap the fingers of your right hand to your forehead.

Train

Slide the index and middle fingers of your right hand over the index and middle fingers of your left hand, both palms facing downward.

Prepositions and Directions

On

Place the palm of your right hand on top of the back of your left hand. This sign can instead be used for *build* or *block*.

Open

Place your palms down with the sides of your index fingers touching and twist your hands upward and outward until your hands are apart and your palms are facing upward.

Actions

Blow

Place your right index finger to your lips (as if to go *shhhh*) and move it outward away from your face. TIP: You can use this sign for bubbles, too.

Bounce

Tap the palms of both hands on the front of your thighs twice.

Build - See On

Help

Place your left fist, thumb on top, in the open palm of your right hand and simultaneously move both hands in an upward direction.

Jump

Place the index and middle fingers of your right hand (inverted "v") on the open palm of your left hand. Move your right hand up and down as if your fingers are jumping.

Swing

Swing the fingers of your right hand over the open upward facing palm of your left hand.

Appendix 3: Oral Motor Songs

For each oral motor exercise, sit across from your child and encourage him to imitate the described movements. As a variation, sit behind your child in front of a mirror and encourage imitation. To be most effective, practice each movement three to 10 times. To make these exercises more functional, practice them before a meal or before a structured language activity.

Like a camel
Chewing leaves
Make your mouth
Chew like me

Instructions: With your teeth together and lips closed, exaggerate chewing movements by moving your jaw from both side-to-side and up and down.

Fishy Fishy
Swimming in the sea
Make a fishy
Face like me

Instructions: Round your lips and make loud kisses. This position helps increase oral motor strength. *Sh, wuh, ch, juh* and *oo* are sounds associated with this position.

Tick tick tock

Like a clock

Make your tongue go

Tick tick tock

Instructions: Move your tongue back and forth (side-to-side) to increase oral motor coordination. Your tongue should not brush your lips.

Clickety-Clack

Clickety-Clack

Make the sound

Of a train on a track

Instructions: Suck your tongue to the top of your mouth and release, keeping your jaw motionless, to make a popping noise. Objective is to strengthen the tongue.

Be the wind

Make a breeze

Make your mouth

Blow like me

Instructions: Take a deep breath and blow, ensuring lips are in an *o* position.

Stretch your tongue
Up to the sky
Pretend it's a rocket-ship
About to fly

Instructions: Stretch your tongue
toward your nose.

Make a happy face
Do not frown
Make a happy face
Like a clown

Instructions: Start out with your lips closed in a neutral position. Gradually draw your lips back to create a wide grin. *M, b* and *p* are sounds associated with a closed lip position.

Peek-a-boo

I see you

Make your tongue play

Peek-a-boo

Instructions: Open your mouth wide and stick your tongue out as far as it will go, then quickly pull it in toward your throat.

Appendix 4: Recommended Book List

Interactive, Sensory, Song, and Character Books

Emma Dodd. *Dog's Birthday A Touch and Feel Book*. Penguin Group (USA) Incorporated, 2006.

Tom Brannon, illus. *Monster Faces*. Random House Books for Young Readers, 1996.

Joy Labrack. *Elmo's Animal Adventures*. Illus. Sue Dicicco. Random House Books for Young Readers, 2000.

Vicky Verbeke. *Chugga Chugga Choo*. Amazon Digital Services, 2013. Kindle edition.

Roger Priddy. *Bright Baby Touch and Feel Perfect Pets*. Priddy Books, 2006.

Keith Faulkner. *Knock Knock*. Illus. Stephen Holmes. Brighter Minds Children's Publishing, 2005.

Simms Taback. *Peek-a-Boo...Who?* Blue Apple, 2006.

Allia Zobel-Nolan. *Eat Your Dinner, Please*. Illus. Michael Terry. Reader's Digest Association, 2003.

Julie Aigner-Clark. *Baby Einstein: Peek-a-Boo Bard*. Illus. Nadeem Zaidi and Madee Zaidi. Hyperion Books for Children, 2005.

David Carter, illus. *If You're Happy And You Know It, Clap Your Hands!* Scholastic, Inc., 1997.

Barney Saltzberg. *A Touch and Feel Book: Peek-a-boo Kisses*. Houghton Mifflin Harcourt, 2002.

Joseph Mathieu, illus. *Elmo's Big Lift-and-Look Book*. Random House Children's Books, 1994.

Nancy Stevenson. *Where's Elmo's Blanket?* Random House Children's Books, 1999.

Gayla Amaral. *Barney's Sing-A-Long Stories: B-I-N-G-O*. Illus. Darren McKee. Scholastic Inc., 2002.

Dena Neusner. *Barney: Sing-A-Long Stories: If You're Happy and You Know It.* Illus. Darren McKee. Scholastic Inc., 2004.

Dena Neusner. *Barney's Sing-A-Long Stories: Clean Up!.* Illus. Darren McKee. Scholastic, 2003.

Nina Laden. *Peek-a Who?* Chronicle Books, 2000.

Book Series

Anne Millard. *Touch and Feel* Series. DK Publishing.

Peek-a-Book Series. DK Publishing.

Movement Books

Lorinda Bryan Cauley. *Clap Your Hands*. G. P. Putnam's Sons, 2001.

Eric Carle. *From Head to Toe Board Book*. Harper Collins Publishers, 1999.

Other Author Favorites

Bill Martin Jr. *Brown Bear, Brown Bear, What Do You See? (Slide and Find)*. Illus. Eric Carle. Priddy Books, 2010.

Bill Martin Jr. *Polar Bear, Polar Bear, What Do You Hear?* Illus. Eric Carle. Henry Holt and Co. (BYR), 1997.

Appendix 5: Daily Checklist

Keeping Track of Opportunities

	S	M	T	W	TH	F	S		S	M	T	W	TH	F	S
Breakfast															
Dressing															
Peer Play															
Snack															
Backyard Play															
Shopping															
Lunch															
TV															
Playground															
Story time															
Dinner															
Bath															
Toileting															
Bedtime															

Ten Tips Summary

- **Tip 1: Do What Does Not Come Naturally** shows you how to give your child a reason to talk.

- **Tip 2: Juice or Milk?** explains how to provide your child with more opportunities to expand his language skills.

- **Tip 3: Simple Signs** explains how you can use sign language to help your child make the connection that language has a purpose.

- **Tip 4: Be Silly** shows you how to incorporate silliness into everyday situations in order to promote listening skills.

- **Tip 5: Talk It Out** explains how verbalizing your own actions or those of your child exposes your child to different aspects of language, speech, and communication.

- **Tip 6: Keep It Moving!** explains how you can use oral motor exercises in order to help your child practice the mouth movements that are vital for speech.

- **Tip 7: The Cow Says Moo** shows you how to help your child find the right word.

- **Tip 8: Break It Down** shows you how to break words down into smaller components so that your child can communicate more effectively.

- **Tip 9: Get Your Groove On** shows you how to pair movement with sound in order to help your child learn language through a sensation other than sound.

- **Tip 10: Books, Books, and More Books** shows you how to incorporate books into your strategy for encouraging language development.

Appendix 6: What is the Early Intervention Program for Infants and Toddlers?

The Early Intervention Program for Infants and Toddlers with Disabilities, also referred to as Part C of the Individuals with Disabilities Education Act (IDEA)[3], is a Federal grant program that is designed to assist states in operating a statewide comprehensive program of early intervention services for eligible infants and toddlers (birth until three years of age), and their families. This program was established by Congress in 1986 to enhance the development of children under the age of three with disabilities, augment a family's ability to meet their child's needs, lessen the possibility of institutionalization, maximize independent living, and decrease educational costs by reducing the need for special education in later years.

Direct services are provided in the child's natural environment and generally include, but are not limited to, developmental intervention, speech and language therapy, occupational therapy, physical therapy, family training, and nursing services. Currently, all states and eligible territories are participating in this program.

Despite being a federal program, statewide early intervention systems vary from state to state because states are permitted some discretion in setting the criteria for child eligibility. As a result, some states serve children at risk for developing a delay, while others serve only those with disabilities.

States also differ concerning which state agency has been designated lead agency. In New Hampshire and West Virginia, for example, the Department of Health and Human Services oversees the program. In states such as Maine, Maryland, Iowa, and Oklahoma, Part C is the responsibility of the Department of Education.

Another way in which the program varies between states pertains to family cost participation[4]. While the Federal government dictates that evaluation, assessment,

---

[3] http://mailcenter3.comcast.net/wm/idea/Idea.asp

[4] A term used to describe a system of payments, including a sliding fee scale, the use of private insurance, or both.

procedural safeguards must be provided at no cost to the family, there is no such mandate for direct services. Though some early intervention recipients might receive services at no cost, others might receive services only through family cost participation.

Appendix 7: Listings by State and Territory

Alabama

Alabama Department of Rehabilitative Services

1-800-543-3098 Toll Free Child Find

1-866-450-2838 Toll Free Spanish

http://rehab.alabama.gov/individuals-and-families/early-intervention/about-alabama's-early-intervention-system

Alaska

Alaska Infant Learning Program

1-877-477-3659 Toll Free

1-907-269-8442

http://dhss.alaska.gov/ocs/Pages/infantlearning/default.aspx

Arizona

Arizona Early Intervention Program (AzEIP)

1-602-532-9960

1-888-439-5609 Toll Free in Arizona

https://www.azdes.gov/main.aspx?menu=98&id=3026

Arkansas

First Connections

1-800-643-8258 Toll Free

http://humanservices.arkansas.gov/ddds/Pages/FirstConnectionsProgram.aspx

Bureau of Indian Education

1-919-962-2001 Main Number

http://ectacenter.org/topics/bie/bie.asp

California

Early Start

1-916- 654-1690 California Department of Developmental Service Main Number

http://specialchildren.about.com/gi/o.htm?zi=1/XJ&zTi=1&sdn=specialchildren&cdn=parenting&tm=113&f=00&su=p284.13.342.ip_p504.6.342.ip_&tt=2&bt=0&bts=0&zu=http%3A//www.dds.ca.gov/earlystart/

Colorado

Early Intervention Colorado

1-888-777-4041 Toll Free Main Number

http://www.eicolorado.org/

Connecticut

Birth to Three System

1-866-888-4188 Toll Free Family Support Line

http://www.birth23.org/

Delaware

Birth to Three Early Intervention System

1-302-255-9134 Main Number

http://www.dhss.delaware.gov/dms/epqc/birth3/directry.html

District of Columbia

DC Early Intervention Program

1-202-727-3665

http://osse.dc.gov/service/dc-early-intervention-program

Florida

Florida Directory of Early Childhood Services

1-800-654-4440 Toll Free Central Directory

http://www.centraldirectory.org/index.cfm

Georgia

Babies Can't Wait (BCW)

1-800-229-2038 Toll Free BCW Directory

1-404-657-2726 State BCW Office

1-888-651-8224 Toll Free State BCW Office

http://health.state.ga.us/programs/bcw/index.asp

Hawaii

H-Kiss

1-808-594-0066 for Oahu

1-800-235-5477 Toll Free for Neighbor Islands

http://hawaii.gov/health/family-child-health/family-child-health/eis/index.html

Idaho

Idaho Infant Toddler Program

2-1-1 or 1-800-926-2588 for Idaho CareLine

http://www.healthandwelfare.idaho.gov/Children/InfantToddlerProgram/tabid/78/Default.aspx

Illinois

Illinois Department of Human Services Early Intervention Program

1-217-782-1981, Option 1

http://www.dhs.state.il.us/ei/

Indiana

First Steps

1-800-545-7763 Toll Free

http://www.in.gov/fssa/4655.htm

Iowa

Early Access

1-888-IAKIDS1 Toll Free

http://www.earlyaccessiowa.org/

Kansas

Kansas Infant-Toddler Services

1-785-296-6135 Main Number

1-800- 332-6262 Toll Free Main Number

http://www.kdheks.gov/its/

Kentucky

First Steps

1-877-417-8377 or 1-877-41 STEPS Toll Free

http://chfs.ky.gov/dph/firststeps.htm

Louisiana

EarlySteps

1-225- 342-0095 Central Office

http://new.dhh.louisiana.gov/index.cfm/page/139/n/139

Maine

Child Development Services

1-877-770-8883 Toll Free

http://www.maine.gov/education/speced/cds/index.htm

Maryland

Division of Special Education/Early Intervention Services

1-410-767-0234

http://www.marylandpublicschools.org/MSDE/divisions/earlyinterv/

Massachusetts

Division for Perinatal, Early Childhood, and Special Health Needs/Early Intervention Program

1-617-624-5901

http://www.nectac.org/shortURL.asp?sURL=MA-partC

Michigan

Early On

1-800-Early-On (1-800-327-5966)

http://www.1800earlyon.org/

Minnesota

Infant and Toddler Intervention

1-651-582-8473

http://www.nectac.org/shortURL.asp?sURL=MN-partC

Mississippi

First Steps

1-800-451-3903 Toll Free

http://www.msdh.state.ms.us/msdhsite/index.cfm/41,0,74,html

Missouri

First Steps

1-866-583-2392 Toll Free

http://dese.mo.gov/divspeced/FirstSteps/index.html

Montana

Developmental Disabilities Program

1-406-444-2995 Main Number

http://www.dphhs.mt.gov/dsd/

Nebraska

Early Development Network

1-402-471-2471

1-888-806-6287 Toll Free

http://edn.ne.gov/

Nevada

Early Intervention Services

1-800-522-0066 Toll Free Project ASSIST

http://www.nectac.org/shortURL.asp?sURL=NV-partC

New Hampshire

Family Centered Early Supports and Services (ESS)

1-603-224-7005 Parent Information Center

1-800- 947-7005 Toll Free Parent Information Center

http://www.nhspecialed.org/ESSOverview.shtml

New Jersey

New Jersey Early Intervention System (NJEIS)

1-888-653-4463 Toll Free

http://nj.gov/health/fhs/eis/index.shtml

New Mexico

Family Infant Toddler (FIT) Program

1-877-696-1472 Toll Free

http://nmhealth.org/ddsd/nmfit/

New York

New York State Early Intervention Program

1-518-473-7016 Bureau of Early Intervention

http://www.health.ny.gov/community/infants_children/early_intervention/

North Carolina

North Carolina Infant Toddler Program (NC ITP)

919-707-5520

http://www.ncei.org/ei/index.html

North Dakota

North Dakota Department of Human Services/Early Intervention

1-701-328-8936 Program Administrator

http://www.nd.gov/dhs/services/disabilities/earlyintervention/

Ohio

Help Me Grow

1-800-755-4769 (GROW) Toll Free

http://www.ohiohelpmegrow.org/About%20Us/abouthelpmegrow.aspx

Oklahoma

Sooner Start

2-1-1- Joint Oklahoma Information Network

http://www.ok.gov/health/County_Health_Departments/Carter_County_Health_Department/SoonerStart_Early_Intervention/index.html

Oregon

Early Intervention Programs

503-947-5747 Oregon Department of Education

http://www.ode.state.or.us/search/results/?id=252

Pennsylvania
Early Intervention Services

1-800-692-7288 Toll Free CONNECT Helpline

http://www.portal.state.pa.us/portal/server.pt/community/early_intervention/87
10

Puerto Rico

Puerto Rico Department of Health: Early Intervention Program

1-787- 274-5660

http://www.familyconnect.org/directory.asp?Action=profile&AccountID=1323

Rhode Island

Early Intervention Program

1-401- 462-0318 Lead Agency

http://www.dhs.ri.gov/ChildrenwithSpecialNeeds/EarlyInterventionProgram/tab
id/839/Default.aspx

South Carolina

BabyNet

1-877-621-0865 Toll Free

http://www.scfirststeps.org/babynet.html

South Dakota

Birth to 3 Connections

1-605-773-3678

1-800-305-3064 Toll Free

http://doe.sd.gov/oess/Birthto3.aspx

Tennessee

Tennessee Early Intervention System (TEIS)

1-800-852-7157 Toll Free

http://www.tn.gov/education/teis/

Texas

Early Childhood Intervention Services

1-800-628-5115 Toll Free

http://www.dars.state.tx.us/ecis/index.shtml

Utah

Baby Watch Early Intervention

1-800-961-4226 Toll Free

http://www.utahbabywatch.org

Vermont

Children's Integrated Services

1-802-769-2194 Early Intervention Administrator

http://dcf.vermont.gov/cdd/cis/IDEA_Part_C_early_intervention

Virgin Islands

US Virgin Islands Infants and Toddlers Early Intervention Program

1-340-777-8804 x 2629 St. Thomas

1-340-773-1311 x 3124 St. Croix

http://www.healthvi.org/programs/family-health/infants-toddlers/index.html

Virginia

Infant & Toddler Connection of Virginia

1-800-234-1448 Toll Free

http://www.infantva.org/

Washington

Early Support for Infants and Toddlers (ESIT)

1-800-322-2588 Toll Free Family Health Hotline

http://del.wa.gov/development/esit/Default.aspx

West Virginia

WV Birth to Three

1-866-321-4728 Toll Free

http://www.wvdhhr.org/birth23/

Wisconsin

Birth to 3 Program

1-608-261-7820 Dept. of Health and Family Services Main Number

http://www.dhs.wisconsin.gov/children/birthto3/index.htm

Wyoming

Early Intervention and Education Unit

1-307-777-7115
http://www.health.wyo.gov/ddd/earlychildhood/index.html

Appendix 8: Listings for Canada

Public Health Agency of Canada

The Division of Childhood and Adolescence of the Public Health Agency of Canada provides program information related to parenting, children's health and well-being, parenting, and newborn care.

Division of Childhood and Adolescence

1-613-952-1220

http://www.phac-aspc.gc.ca/hp-ps/dca-dea/about-apropos/index-eng.php

Canadian Paediatric Society

The Canadian Paediatric Society is the national association of paediatricians. They publish an early childhood development resource list for Canadian provinces and territories.

Early Childhood Development/Provincial/Territorial and Community Resources

http://www.cps.ca/en/issues-questions/early-childhood-development-resources

Provincial and Territorial Early Intervention Programs

Support for Early Intervention programs in Canada varies. Quebec, Alberta, Ontario, Nova Scotia, Prince Edward Island, and British Columbia all cover some of the costs associated with early intervention therapy. However, for some provinces, wait-lists are extensive and services fragmented.

British Columbia

Ministry of Children and Family Development

1-250 952-6044 Children and Youth with Special Needs Main Number

http://www.mcf.gov.bc.ca/spec_needs/eci.htm

Quebec

Quebec Society for Disabled Children

1-877-937-6171 Toll Free

http://www.enfantshandicapes.com/en/who-we-are/mission-and-history.html

Alberta

Child and Family Services Authority

1-780-427-2250 Main Number

http://www.edmontonandareacfsa.gov.ab.ca/publish/517.cfm

Manitoba

Healthy Child Manitoba

1-888-848-0140 Toll Free Main Number

http://www.gov.mb.ca/healthychild/ecd/index.html

New Brunswick

Premier's Council on the Status of Disabled Person/Early Intervention Program

1-506-454-8698 ext. 106

http://www.gnb.ca/0048/PCSDP/DirectoriesForPersons/DirectoryofServices/Alphabeticalndex/E-e.asp

Newfoundland

Newfoundland Labrador Department of Health and Community Services

1-709-729-3193 Program Consultant for Intervention Services

http://www.health.gov.nl.ca/health/personsdisabilities/index.html

Northwest Territories

Early Childhood and School Services

http://www.ece.gov.nt.ca/contact-us Phone Contacts by Region

http://www.ece.gov.nt.ca/early-childhood-and-school-services/early-childhood

Nova Scotia

Early Intervention Program

http://www.gov.ns.ca/coms/department/contact/index.html Phone Contacts by Region

http://www.earlyintervention.net/

Ontario

Infant and Child Development Programs

http://www.oaicd.ca/icd Phone Contacts by Region

http://www.oaicd.ca/

Prince Edward Island

Children's Secretariat

http://www.gov.pe.ca/photos/original/edu_childsec09.pdf Phone Contacts

Family Place

1-902-436-1348

http://www.peifamilyplace.com/

Early Childhood Development Association of PEI

1-888-368-1866 Toll Free

http://earlychildhooddevelopment.ca/index.php?q=node/27

Saskatchewan

Early Childhood Development and Integrated Services

1-306-787-6532

http://www.education.gov.sk.ca/ECIP

Yukon

Yukon Youth and Social Services Family and Children's Services

1-800-661-0408 Toll Free Health and Social Services Main Number

http://www.hss.gov.yk.ca/family_children.php

Child Development Centre

1-866-835-8386 Toll Free

http://www.cdcyukon.com/aboutus/missionvision.html

Made in the USA
Monee, IL
29 April 2021